GREAT
ENGINEERING

BUILDING

SKYSCRAPERS

REBECCA STEFOFF

Cavendish Square

New York

Published in 2016 by Cavendish Square Publishing, LLC
243 5th Avenue, Suite 136, New York, NY 10016

Copyright © 2016 by Cavendish Square Publishing, LLC

First Edition

Website: cavendishsq.com

This publication represents the opinions and views of the author based on his or her personal experience, knowledge, and research. The information in this book serves as a general guide only. The author and publisher have used their best efforts in preparing this book and disclaim liability rising directly or indirectly from the use and application of this book.

CPSIA Compliance Information: Batch #WS15CSQ

All websites were available and accurate when this book was sent to press.

Library of Congress Cataloging-in-Publication Data

Stefoff, Rebecca.
Building skyscrapers / by Rebecca Stefoff.
p. cm. — (Great engineering)
Includes index.
ISBN 978-1-50260-607-5 (hardcover) ISBN 978-1-50260-606-8 (paperback)
ISBN 978-1-50260-608-2 (ebook)
1. Skyscrapers — Juvenile literature. 2. Skyscrapers — Design and construction — Juvenile literature.
I. Stefoff, Rebecca, 1951-. II. Title.

NA6230.S74 2016

720'.483—d23

Editorial Director: David McNamara
Editor: Andrew Coddington
Copy Editor: Rebecca Rohan
Art Director: Jeffrey Talbot
Designer: Amy Greenan
Senior Production Manager: Jennifer Ryder-Talbot
Production Editor: Renni Johnson
Photo Research: J8 Media

Printed in the United States of America

TABLE OF CONTENTS

CHAPTER ONE

Going Up

Cities are like living things. They change and grow.

Cities get bigger when the number of people living in them goes up. Sometimes this happens when the people who live in the city have children. Sometimes new people move to the city from other places. Many of them come to look for jobs.

All of these people need places to live, work, go to

Chicago was one of the first cities to have skyscrapers. Today, it is home to many tall buildings.

school, and shop. The city has to grow to make room for them. Where will people put the new homes and buildings they need?

How a City Grows

A city can grow by spreading out. New streets and neighborhoods rise up on the edges of the old city.

This old map shows Manhattan, the heart of New York City. Manhattan is an island with water on all sides. Builders had to go up, not out.

They become part of the city. In time, more streets and neighborhoods are built. They are even farther out. The city gets bigger and bigger.

Sometimes a city hits a limit. It cannot keep growing in all directions. Maybe the city sits on the edge of the ocean or has a river on one side. Maybe a swamp or a mountain keeps the city from spreading.

If a city *can* just keep growing outward, it may get huge. The newest parts of the city will be very far from the center. People who live on the edge and work in the center would have to travel a long way every day.

There is one way a city can grow even if rivers and mountains are in its way. It can get bigger without always spreading outward. A city can grow upward.

Tall Buildings

People have been building tall **structures** for a long time. The Great Pyramid of Giza in Egypt was built more than four thousand years ago. It is 479 feet (146 meters) high. For more than three thousand years it was the tallest thing built by humans in the world.

The Great Pyramid was the burial place of a king. It was not made

Egypt's Great Pyramid was the tallest human-made structure in the world for more than three thousand years—but it was not a skyscraper.

for people to live in. Other tall structures in the ancient world were built for people to live in. They were **habitable**.

Two thousand years ago the city of Rome, Italy, had apartment buildings ten **stories** high. One thousand years ago Egyptian cities had buildings of fourteen stories. The lower floors held shops. The upper floors were apartments where people lived.

Not Too High!

Tall buildings were one answer to the problem of growing cities. But tall buildings had two big problems of their own.

First, think about living on the fourteenth floor. To reach your room you would have to climb up, and up, and up. People lived on the high floors because they had no choice. Still, there was a limit. No one wanted to climb thirty or forty flights of stairs.

Old buildings in Edinburgh, Scotland. Crowded cities had stone "high-rises." Some old apartment buildings were more than twice this high.

Second, stone or brick buildings needed thick walls to hold up their weight. For a building to reach fifteen stories, the walls on the lower levels had to be very, very thick. This made the rooms too small for shops or apartments.

The answer to these problems was the **skyscraper**.

CHAPTER TWO

What Is a Skyscraper?

Not just any building can be called a skyscraper. A skyscraper has to be habitable. It also has to rise higher than a lot of the buildings in the same city.

How tall does a building have to be to be called a skyscraper? The answer depends on where and when it was built.

Manhattan today is full of towering buildings. Streets are like valleys between them.

In 1885, a new building opened in Chicago. It was ten stories tall. That building towered over everything around it. It was a skyscraper in its day.

Today a ten-story building would not be called a skyscraper. Now a building needs to be 330 feet (100 meters) tall—or taller—to be a skyscraper. A lot of skyscrapers are much, much taller.

Two Secrets to Building Skyscrapers

Do you remember the two problems with tall buildings?
One problem was too many stairs. The other problem was thick walls of stone or brick. New inventions solved those problems.

In 1853, this elevator was a brand-new invention.

The invention of the **elevator** solved the problem of too many stairs. An elevator is a box big enough to hold people. It moves up and down inside a building on cables, or strong ropes made of steel. After elevators were invented in 1852, people did not have to climb to the top floors of tall buildings.

Steel also solved the problem of thick walls. A frame made of **beams**, or long pieces of steel, can hold up a building from the inside, like a skeleton. It takes much less space than huge blocks of stone. Thin walls of brick or even glass can hang from the frame. This kind of wall is called a **curtain wall**. It is the outer "skin" of a skyscraper.

The Home Insurance Building in Chicago was the world's first skyscraper. At first, buildings like this were called "cloud-scrapers."

Planning a Skyscraper

The ten-story building that opened in Chicago in 1885 used this new kind of **construction**, with a frame and curtain walls.

It started an age of skyscraper building in Chicago, New York, and other cities.

All skyscrapers start with a plan. **Architects** and **engineers** work together to plan skyscrapers.

Architects design buildings. They decide how buildings will look and how the space inside them will be divided into rooms.

Engineers are experts in how to build things and in what materials to use. They know how much weight steel can hold and how long it takes **concrete** to dry.

Engineers turn ideas or plans into real structures. They tell an architect if a design can be built—or if it needs to be changed. They make sure the design will stand up to high winds. Wind puts a lot of pressure on skyscrapers.

Planning a skyscraper takes a team. A **geologist** might be part of the team. Geologists study the

Architects study a model of a building they are planning.

earth. They can tell whether the ground will support the skyscraper.

Together the team draws a plan. They also build small models to show how the building will look.

Everyone has to agree on the plan. The company that is paying for the building has to like it. The city where it is being built has to say yes, too. Then it is time to start work.

CHAPTER THREE

A Tall Job

A skyscraper reaches for the sky. Before engineers build it, they must burrow into the earth.

Tall buildings need strong foundations, the bottom layers that hold everything up. For a skyscraper, the foundation goes down into the ground.

Digging Down

Workers dig a big hole where the skyscraper will stand. They use special machines to move large amounts of earth.

One important machine is called an excavator.

It moves on tracks, like a tank. The driver of the excavator steers a big scoop on a long arm. It reaches out and grabs a load of dirt, then dumps it into a truck to be carried away.

For the tallest skyscrapers, the excavation goes all the way down to solid rock. Other skyscrapers stand on hard clay.

Building the Frame

A skyscraper's frame is made out of steel beams. The up-and-down beams are called **columns**. The side-to-side beams are **girders**.

Steel beams fastened to concrete pads hold up the bottom of the skyscraper.

Beams used to be fastened together by thousands of steel bolts called **rivets**. Today builders still use some rivets, but they also fasten metal pieces together with hot, melted metal. This is called **welding**.

Many skyscrapers look like a set of big "steps" as they go up. The bottom may cover a whole city block, but the top is not as wide. Those "steps" are called **setbacks**. Setbacks make the top part of the skyscraper weigh less. They also let more light and air reach the street.

Builders work from the foundation upward. First the columns for each level are set in place. Then the girders are fastened to the columns. Once a few levels are done, some workers start hanging the curtain walls on the frame. Other workers keep building the frame upward.

High above the ground, a skyscraper construction worker stands on a platform called a scaffold. He is roped to the scaffold in case of a fall. The "steps" built into the skyscraper behind him are setbacks.

Hanging the Walls

The outer "skin" of a skyscraper can be made of many things. Curtain walls can be made of glass, thin sheets of stone, or metals that are light but strong. Many buildings use all three materials.

The mirrored walls of skyscrapers are pretty. Sometimes, though, they aim a lot of heat at the street.

A lot of modern skyscrapers have outer walls that are mostly glass. Sometimes the glass is made to work like a mirror. A person standing on the street may see clouds drifting across the face of the skyscraper. The building is a big mirror that reflects the sky.

As the curtain wall is put in place, workers start constructing the inside of the building. They put floors and ceilings on the web of girders. They build walls to separate the rooms and hallways.

The tall, narrow shafts that will hold the elevators are built at this time. Skyscrapers need a lot of elevators. Some elevators only go to the highest floors.

When the frame and the curtain walls are done, the inside of the skyscraper can be finished. Bathrooms, lights, and carpets are put in. Inspectors check to make sure everything works. They also check the safety equipment, such as fire alarms. Once everything is ready, people and businesses move into the new skyscraper.

CHAPTER FOUR

Reaching for the Sky

Why do people build skyscrapers?

The taller a building is, the more people and businesses can fit on the same piece of land. At one time, a hotel called the Waldorf Astoria filled a city block in New York. Part of the hotel was thirteen stories tall. Part was seventeen stories tall. It had restaurants and rooms for travelers.

Today the Empire State Building stands on that same block. When the Empire State Building was

finished in 1931, it was the tallest building in the world. It was almost forty years before a taller building was built.

The Empire State Building has 103 stories. Many, many more people use that city block now than when it was a hotel.

People also build skyscrapers just because they can. Architects and engineers love the challenge of creating a tall tower. The companies and governments that pay for skyscrapers take pride in their huge structures.

Countries and cities that have the world's biggest buildings are proud of them, too. Super-tall buildings draw visitors from around the world.

The Burj Khalifa was the tallest building in the world in 2015—but for how long?

The World's Tallest Buildings

A group called the Council on Tall Buildings and Urban Habitat keeps track of skyscrapers around the world. It studies the way these huge buildings change cities. It also keeps a list of the world's tallest buildings.

At the beginning of 2015, the tallest building was the Burj Khalifa. Its name means "Khalifa Tower" in Arabic. This structure rises above the city of Dubai in the Middle East.

The Burj Khalifa was finished in 2010. It is 2,723 feet (830 meters) tall. But the top of the building is a tall spire, or point. Only 1,918 feet (585 meters) of the Burj Kjalifa is habitable. That part houses offices, a hotel, and apartments on 163 floors.

The second tallest building in the world is the Makkah Royal Clock Tower Hotel in Saudi Arabia. Like the Burj Khalifa, it has a spire. With the spire, the building is 1,972 feet (601 meters) tall. Without the spire, the part that is habitable is 1,833 feet (559 meters) tall.

One World Trade Center in New York City is the third tallest building in the world. With its spire it is 1,792 feet (546 meters) tall. The habitable part is 1,268 feet (387 meters) tall. One World Trade Center has ninety-four floors above the ground, five floors below the ground, and seventy-three elevators.

The next six tallest buildings in the world are all in Asia. In fact, Asia has most of the fifty tallest buildings. The United States has seven. Russia has one of the fifty tallest buildings.

The Future of Skyscrapers

Buildings even taller than the Burj Khalifa are already being planned. Some are being built. In Saudi Arabia, work has started on the Kingdom Tower. When it is finished, it will be 3,281 feet (1,000 meters) tall.

The skyscrapers of the future may look different from those of today. Architects and engineers are always coming up with new ideas.

One idea is the garden wall. Gardens hanging on

An architect's idea for a future skyscraper shaped like an arch. Plants on the building help clean the air. This skyscraper makes its own energy from the sun and wind.

the outer walls of skyscrapers could help clean the air. They could also be used to grow food. Another idea is the energy farm. Windmills and solar panels on skyscrapers already make energy for some buildings.

And who says skyscrapers have to go up in a straight line? Future structures could be shaped like wings, or arches. One thing is certain: the builders of skyscrapers will keep reaching for the sky.

GLOSSARY

architect Someone trained to design buildings.

beam A long piece of steel used in making skyscraper frames.

column A beam pointing up that is part of a skyscraper frame.

concrete A blend of sand, gravel, cement, and water that is hard and strong when it dries.

construction The act of building, or constructing.

curtain wall The outer "skin" of a skyscraper, a thin wall of brick, glass, or metal that hangs from an inner frame of steel.

elevator A machine that raises and lowers a compartment in a hollow tube, or shaft, inside a building; the compartment can carry people or goods.

engineer Someone who uses science and math to plan and build things.

geologist A scientist who studies geology, the subject of the earth and what it is made of.

girder A beam laid sideways in a skyscraper frame.

habitable Able to be lived in, or used.

rivet A steel bolt used to fasten pieces of metal together.

setback A place where the skyscraper has a "step" built into it; the part above the setback is not as wide as the part below it.

skyscraper Any building that is habitable all the way from ground level to the top story, and taller than most buildings around it.

story, stories A level or floor in a building, or the number of levels.

structure Something built by humans, such as a building, tower, or bridge.

welding Using hot, melted metal to fasten two pieces of metal together.

FIND OUT MORE

Books

Cornille, Didier. *Who Built That? Skyscrapers: An Introduction to Skyscrapers and Their Architects.* New York: Princeton Architectural Press, 2014.

Hopkinson, Deborah. *Sky Boys: How They Built the Empire State Building.* New York: Schwartz and Wade, 2012.

Latham, Donna. *Skyscrapers.* White River Junction, VT: Nomad Press, 2013.

Websites

Building Big: All About Skyscrapers

www.pbs.org/wgbh/buildingbig/skyscraper/

How Skyscrapers Work

www.howstuffworks.com/engineering/structural/skyscraper.htm

INDEX

ABOUT THE AUTHOR

Rebecca Stefoff has written books for young readers on many topics in science, technology, and history. She is the author of the six-volume series Is It Science? (Cavendish Square, 2014) and the four-volume series Animal Behavior Revealed (Cavendish Square, 2014). She also wrote *The Telephone*, *The Camera*, *Submarines*, *The Microscope and Telescope*, and *Robots* for Cavendish Square's Great Inventions series. Stefoff lives in Portland, Oregon. You can learn more about Stefoff and her books for young people at www.rebeccastefoff.com.